An Insightful Journal for the Spiritual Journey

1111

AWAKEN

©2020 by Roni Hopkins
All rights reserved.
ISBN: 978-1-7349035-0-8

JOURNALS OF REALIZATION

"The only truth one could ever die for is the truth they themselves have become"

Roni Hopkins is the creator of *Journals of Realization*, which are a collection of unique journals that specialize in spirituality and consciousness. She has traveled the world, connecting with all walks of life and lives her purpose dedicated to assisting others on their journey. The creation of these journals reflect those experiences and bring a level of universal insight to ones own spiritual path. Journals of Realization encourages you to discover and express your truth, wisdom and ever evolving awareness throughout the pages and beyond them through our virtual discussions.

Every path reveals its truth within you.

www.RoniHopkins.com

PREFACE

If you were able to consciously remove yourself from the titles, the obligations and expectations of all the ideas of what "being" human is:

What would be left of your life, your identity, your existence?

Would you perceive yourself as an individual separate from the whole?

Spiritual awakening is simply when one begins to become aware of the spirit nature and their eternal being within the sphere of time, space and this physical plane.

This state of enlightenment propels a transformation that redefines identities, understandings, beliefs and truths that once defined us and our life.

It is a process of being reborn from the inside out.

You see and understand the true nature of life and all that lives and breathes around you. You become connected to life through a much different bond and are in tune with your purpose and experience in it.

The journey begins when you are open to see what you could not see before. The discovery of this eternal existence is the spiritual journey within yourself.

When we ask: "Who Am I ?" and seek to understand the answer beyond this physical life, the unveiling leads to an expansive unfolding of all of life itself.

This is your Spiritual Journey

From Pen to Paper

Your Thoughts

Your Experiences

Your Realizations

"How we see ourselves in this physical plane is only a fraction of the true reality of our existence. Once the unveiling begins, be open to all that you possibly are"

Our spirit nature is our divinity. It is the connectivity to love, peace, fulfillment, life's purpose and all the areas of our existence that go beyond what our mind and this physical life can create and sustain for us.

It awakens to be discovered.

11 11

11 11

11 11

11 11

11 11

"The Spiritual Journey will take you beyond the depths of any place you could ever imagine here on earth"

It is an endless unveiling of our connection with the realities of all creation itself. The expansion of its horizons are far greater than what could ever be measured.

There is so much beyond this life you will discover and in turn life will begin to mirror all that you are.

Everything changes as you become everything.

11 11

11 11

11 11

11 11

"Spiritual Consciousness is a state of continuous awareness that expands far beyond this physical realm. It is inexhaustible to be defined as one singular truth. It is the All that everything is"

The idea of being made aware is like observing a tree. You can see the trunk, the color of the leaves and the fullness of its bloom. In one aspect, it is so.

You may also see the leaves and perceive an understanding of plant cell cycles, photosynthesis and how each leaf though similar in nature are different.

Spiritual Awareness:

Being able to comprehend beyond the physical and gather understanding outside of the limitations of what we perceive as our only reality.

11 11

11 11

11 11

11 11

11 11

Surrender

You are standing at the edge of the ocean
The wind is caressing in and through you
The sun sets in the back drop
The warmth balances the chill in the air
Music plays

Softly

Reminding you to flow
Flow in this moment like lyrics cascading into the notes
In harmony with your breath
Heart beats in stillness
Tears flow there way to the edge of your existence

This is it

The stars appear along the horizon
Gazing upon your *Surrender*
Black is the color of this canvas now
And you weep
Crying out in whispers

I am yours

Wrapping your arms around yourself
Pulling yourself into yourself
Your knees buckle
Your skin shivers in this moment of vulnerability
The ocean shouts in rhythm but distance to be seen

I am infinite

Reaching into the sky as your lovers embrace you yearned for
Consumption fills your chest

Tightness of Inhale

It is happening

You close your eyes
The sea follows your breath into your lungs
Your eyes no longer perceive what they believed
This is your legacy

I am Free

11 11

11 11

11 11

11 11

11 11

"As the existence of all things physical are subject to evolve and change, so are you to ever evolve into what can never be defined as anything"

Your identity is no longer defined as something that holds limitations to your existence.

You are not the same person as you were yesterday and quickly that can be changed in an instant.

You will evolve through time not being confined to the past nor the future.

The present moment of now exist in a state that is always new. There you will observe yourself constantly evolving and becoming the experiences of life.

11 11

11 11

11 11

60

11 11

"Trust beyond what you can see until you no longer need to see anything at all"

Trusting beyond what you see has always been part of the foundation of becoming aware of the eternal aspect of our existence.

Your mind has to approach what it cannot see and what it cannot comprehend through trust.

It is the variable that will calm the late night hours and will cease the fears of the outcomes.

It is the bridge that connects divine reality to a mind that has yet to comprehend what it does not know.

11 11

11 11

11 11

"Be content and at peace when things are falling apart as they are actually falling into place"

Spiritual transformation will dismantle the old to make way for the new.

The shifting and changing of your life will set you in motion to operate from a new state of being and to experience life in a way that you have not before.

The letting go of the former is essential to your ability to operate from a state of continual spiritual freedom.

11 11

11 11

11 11

11 11

"Life is never what you think it is as the true nature of life itself is beyond conceivable thoughts."

The spiritual journey is far beyond a destination or any set of beliefs or knowledge it can be defined as.

You will simply evolve through life that far exceeds knowledge or understanding but pure creation of what is and what continues to unfold before you as something new.

The evolution itself is the continuous state of becoming and just when you think you have the answers of understanding

It changes like the wind

It flows like the oceans

It transforms your life like a controlled fire

11 11

Breathe

Deeply take it all in
The renewal of Spirit
And the release of the past
Beginnings of a new era daily
For you are a continuous of All
And limitless to freedom

Breathe

Deeply take in the universe
The beyond
The Life that carries you
Grounds you
And keeps you alive
For what is alive, when there is not death
What is death, when all is eternal
Feel your being expanding
Stretching itself into the edges of the universe

It is beautiful
It is effortless

Your physical mind reaches its breaking barriers
But all is well
And all will continue
Nothing releases life like the breath

So Breathe

Release the tension of the expansion
Inhale the renewal of a new way of being

A new Era
A new Life

11 11

11 11

11 11

11 11

11 11

"The Spiritual Journey will evolve you from a state of Learning to Becoming"

When you learn a lesson it comes into the mind and many of us try to replicate the lesson in our doing.

Lending to the concept that the mind itself is the engine behind the spiritual being

In time, you can train it to operate from a state of repetitious behavior patterns and re-programming what it has been taught. We repeat this process until change is accomplished.

The mind is limited in its nature to exist. It has to be taught in order to produce results. Your thoughts of change are simply that:

Thoughts

Your Spirit Being Is Absolute

It uses the mind in hindsight to understand that which you have become.

Never having to learn how to obtain spirituality at all but continuously becoming the evolution of the spirit in the present state of oneness.

11 11

11 11

11 11

11 11

11 11

> *"This physical reality is not the only reality there is. Life can be lived through multidimensional points of existence"*

Your external life will transform as quickly as you find yourself transforming from the inside out.

One of the most challenging aspects of the spiritual journey is simply being okay with all the changes it brings and living life differently than what you lived before.

A realization that unlocks an access that often defies the limitations we once perceived as our reality and granting us the ability to approach it with a new perspective.

What is impossible becomes effortless and what we see as finite becomes infinite.

11 11

11 11

11 11

11 11

"Spiritual Awakening is the beginning of a beautiful journey that one can only experience for themselves. No one can walk the path for you. It is yours alone to discover."

Your experience is the only validity that holds true to your beliefs.

Someone else's knowledge, faith and experience does not give you access to that which is only yours to discover.

It is your path.

Your journey to do so.

Trust the guidance within that will pull you towards a greater depth of life, awareness and realization.

11 11

11 11

11 11

11 11

www.ingramcontent.com/pod-product-compliance
Lightning Source LLC
Chambersburg PA
CBHW031116080526
44587CB00011B/1001